COVID-19
2021-2030

China and the US created the Virus for Agenda 21?
RNA-Technology – Vaccine Victims – MERS-CoV –
Population Control; Exposed!

Rebel Press Media

Disclaimer

Our other books

Check out our other books for other unreported news, exposed facts and debunked truths, and more.

Join the exclusive Rebel Press Media Circle!

You will get new updates about the unreported reality delivered in your inbox every Friday.

Sign up here today:

https://campsite.bio/rebelpressmedia

Introduction

'This is a worldwide time bomb: ANY vaccinated individual will ultimately suffer detrimental effects, and autopsy on vaccinated persons confirms that mRNA and spike proteins move to all organs,' says an infectious disease specialist.

Several scientific investigations have decisively discredited the claim that Covid-19 vaccines only reside in muscle tissue, which has persisted for months. Now, an autopsy on a deceased vaccinated person would reveal that the genetic mRNA instructions, similar to the spike protein created by vaccines, propagated throughout the body to all organs. "This means that ultimately ANY vaccinated person will experience serious side effects," said a horrified infectious disease doctor from New Jersey who did not want to be identified for fear of retaliation.

Because this mRNA has converted vaccinated people into permanent "spike factories," the effects will almost certainly be irreversible. As a result, he concludes, "This is a worldwide time bomb."
The autopsy on a Covid-vaccinated man is reported to be the first of its type, revealing that 'viral RNA' was identified in practically all of the deceased 86-year-old man's organs 24 days after his injection.

When there is no Covid and a negative test, an ADE is triggered by a lethal vaccine-virus combination.

The man's health deteriorated after his first Pfizer shot on January 9, necessitating hospitalization after 18 days. He didn't have any clinical Covid symptoms, and his test came back negative as well.

As a result, "no morphological abnormalities related to Covid" were discovered in his body, according to the post-mortem report.

The 86-year-old caught Covid from another patient on the unit, according to medical authorities, but the autopsy shows that the damage to his organs occurred before he was admitted. That leaves just one possible cause: the vaccination. And when the man was infected in the hospital, he didn't stand a chance, suffering from an ADE reaction, which many independent scientists (including Professor Pierre Capel) and specialists have been warning about for months.

Vaccine mRNA produces virus RNA?

'The vaccine was unable to prevent the virus from infecting every organ,' explains Hal Turner, an American radio broadcaster. However, another possibility is that the 'viral RNA' was actually produced by the vaccine mRNA.

Finally, all vaccines approved in the West instruct the body to generate the virus's spike protein. Only this spike protein - purposefully engineered to better connect to human ACE2 receptors - is accountable for all health damage, according to a recent Pfizer study in Japan, and it spreads throughout the body after immunization, even to the brain, as shown in a recent Nature Neuroscience study.

In conclusion, the logical inference is as follows:

* if the body is bursting at the seams with 'viral RNA,' which would have killed the patient

* ... it has been demonstrated that just the spike protein is the virus's harmful component.

* and mRNA vaccines tell the human body to produce that spike protein.

* in a way that makes it stick to human cells even better than viral spike protein.

* The patient died as a result of an ADE brought on by the spike protein.

* He had no Covid-19 when he was admitted with health concerns 18 days after his vaccination, thus it must have come (primarily) from the vaccine.

People who continue to reassure others and themselves that they were "vaccinated months ago and have nothing to worry about" should remember that the repercussions of these intentional DNA modifications

5

are similar to cancer in that they can develop swiftly but also slowly. Only one problem: once it's there, it won't go away on its own.

Are vaccines already having an impact on judgment?

We just wrote, 'Have nothing to worry about' Is it possible, however, for some persons who have been vaccinated to do so? I got a message from an acquaintance who said he had attempted everything he could to keep two of his pals from getting the vaccine. But it was in vain. Both pals were vaccinated notwithstanding; one is now continually racing, and the other had to be hospitalized due to serious thrombosis (anonymized info published with permission).

And, you guessed it, the doctors involved declared that it couldn't possibly be linked to the vaccine even before the diagnosis and examination. And, strangely enough, the victims believed it as well. Of course, this is all conjecture, but could this inability to think clearly, make sound decisions, and draw conclusions be the result of brain damage induced by those same vaccines?

'Time bomb on a global scale'

When he saw the postmortem report, an infectious disease specialist in New Jersey claimed he was stunned. 'People believe that only a small percentage of vaccine recipients experience side effects. Because these spike proteins attach to ACE2 receptors all across your body, this study suggests that everyone will ultimately experience negative effects.'

'That mRNA should have stayed where it was injected, but it didn't. As a result, the spike proteins produced by the mRNA will end up in every organ. And we know that the damage is caused by this spike protein.'

Table of Contents

Chapter 1: Genetically modified vaccines

'How six months of Fake News absolutely affects you' - What is the 'logic' behind the PCR test and the allegedly increased incidence of 'infections'? : 'The earth is round, and so is a pancake. As a result, the world is a pancake' - The Oxford Covid vaccine was developed in human embryonic kidney cells that had been genetically engineered.

Professor (em.) of Immunology Pierre Capel starts his latest YouTube 'course' with the idea that' six months of Fake News can utterly transform you.' If you were asked a year ago if you would be genetically modified because you were terrified of getting the flu, what would you say? What do you believe your response was? But, after six months of Fake News, you've changed your mind and said, "Yes, please!" But do you know what viral genetic modification is? No, I have no idea, but 'it's our only hope, right?'

Capel also cites an official WHO bulletin from October 14, 2020, claiming that the IFR (mortality rate among the sick) for the entire population up to the age of 70 is only 0.05 percent, and corona is the same as seasonal flu, even among the elderly.

(Of course, the corporate media is spitting forth a new dose of terror today, proclaiming in big headlines that "between March and June, 168,000 more people died in the EU than projected." Simply look at the official

European statistics on EuroMOMO (especially the red dotted line with 'substantial increase') and you'll see that this is yet another deceptive, blatantly manipulative headline designed to keep you in a constant state of panic so that you don't think about what's really going on. It's not a big concern if there's a virus outbreak.

"We're going to talk about something that didn't exist, notably the second wave," Capel says. He refers to the official figures, which show that there were no more registered Covid patients at the end of June. Then folks went mad with PCR testing. Then you witness a massive outbreak of 'infections,' but is this really true? If this were true, there should be a significant increase in the number of persons who die. However, there isn't any.'

From a common pandemic to a bogus case outbreak

We had an epidemic that went on like the flu and passed until June; after June, we had a 'case epidemic,' which is an epidemic of purely positive PCR tests that, as you know, cannot show any virus, yield 94 percent false positives, and thus say nothing about whether someone is infected, let alone sick.

The image was the same in all countries: in the spring, we experienced "a typical seasonal viral respiratory infection," which happens every year. Covid-19 follows the same pattern as Covid-1 through 18. 'At the moment, there are very few hospital and ICU admissions, as well as very few deaths.' The PCR test is the sole way to identify the second wave.'

Then, in his trademark simple, accessible manner for anyone with a year or more of high school, he explains how a PCR test works technically. Essentially, the PCR test (by nose/throat swab) takes a small amount of RNA and exponentially amplifies it: after 35 rounds, 1 metaphorical molecule has been increased by half a billion times. Typically, one would end after 20 rounds.

The Second Wave of last year was made up entirely of useless and unproven 'infections.'

When you consider how many tests are now being performed at the same time, you can see how there is a creation of primers that cannot be lifted to make it fully pure. That's a big task, and it'll cost a lot of money.' The WHO wanted to know whether this is how you show a virus; it is NOT; you only show a small piece of virus - no infection, no live virus.

WHO decided that lengthy testing with three (suspected) virus primers was too expensive and time-consuming, therefore two primers were eliminated, and the third primer was only tested for 35 rounds. A PCR test normally has a multiplier of up to one million. But because there weren't enough positive tests, they increased the number to over half a billion! And if your primers aren't clean, well...'

To put it another way, there was no pandemic, but the government felt compelled to prepare for one regardless. And it was for this reason that the widespread use of PCR tests was set in motion.

First and foremost, the PCR test provides no information regarding the virus's viability. It's just a fragment of RNA that Might be from a virus, but could also be from a virus you had three years ago or something else else. That's where everything gets immunized,' says the narrator. He then displays the official WHO figures once more. The unfortunate reality is that this is Europe.

The number of 'infections,' as they call them, is represented by the blue line. So it's the PCR test that came back positive.' The green (hospitalizations) and red (deaths) lines, on the other hand, do not follow the blue line at all, and have remained largely unchanged for months.

The earth is round, a pancake is round; so the earth is a pancake'.

'Last year's Code Red and lockdown were predicated on the blue line, which just shows how many people were tested.' If we call it a second wave, that is! As a result, a "positive PCR test" has nothing to do with the concept of infection. It's similar to the following equation: 'The world is round, and so is a pancake.' As a result, the earth is a pancake.'

Yes, a few more people became ill with respiratory infections last year, but this happens every year (starting in the fall).

Excess mortality (from influenza, rhino, corona, RSV, and other diseases) was 7500 in 2016-2017, 9400 the following year, and 6130 in 2019-2020. We can now observe that the genuine'second wave' of 2020, based on genuine sick individuals rather than worthless PCR tests, is the first fall wave's typical sick people. What we are looking at in October 2020, is mainly the Rhino virus' (cold virusses).

For a (1.5) meter, social distancing, face masks, and lockdowns did not work.

According to international statistics, all "measures" (1.5 meters, face masks, and lockdowns) are ineffective for a single meter. We could spend hours displaying graphs demonstrating that the (official story) is incorrect. ' According to the media, Sweden, the class's naughty boy, took almost no measures, left everything open, and allowed society go on as usual.' And what do you think you're seeing? 'It's the same gradient,' says the narrator (with even a much lower peak as the countries with the strictest lockdowns, Italy, Great Britain and Spain).

Another clear example is the 47,600 popular pubs in the United Kingdom. It's quite impossible to keep a distance of 1.5 meters there; facemasks aren't used, and ventilation is frequently poor. With an average of 1,000 connections per bar every week, the total number of 'bad' contacts is staggering: 618,800,000 every week. What effect does this have on the number of sick and dead people? ZERO. There is no effect at all! If facemasks and 1.5 meters were truly effective, the number of sick and dead would have skyrocketed. Nothing, however, transpired.

After that, he displays a video of a test he conducted with numerous face masks. It is obvious that all versions worn by the general public are as porous as a sieve. There is no detectable effect in the statistics in nations that have made facemasks mandatory, such as Poland and Austria. As a result, facemasks are useless.

And what about the one-and-a-half meters? Nothing could be further from the truth.' For months, there has been a yes-or-no debate about whether large or little droplets are better (aerosols). Aerosols play a key role, according to a 2010 RIVM study. In that instance, you must maintain a distance of 10 meters rather than 1.5 meters. That makes no sense at all. Social distancing destroys the whole of society, but it doesn't make any difference to Covid.'

Measures are ineffective against viruses, but they are effective for fear.

Fog droplets are significantly larger than aerosols, yet do you observe them falling down within 1.5 meters when traveling through the forest? No! Aerosols float in the air. The importance of ventilation cannot be overstated. Outside, the issues are minor, and after the epidemic is ended, the difficulties inside are minor (but are related to ventilation).'

'As a result, we can tell that the virus's countermeasures are ineffective.' But what exactly do they do? On dread! On people's actions and social interactions. Everything is ruined!' In the less rich countries, it produces widespread poverty and other misery (mass unemployment, vast numbers of sick individuals). 'They are now dying like rats in nations like India and Indonesia. "But hey, as long as it's not here," Capel sarcastically adds.

'It's not a vaccine; SARS-CoV-2 protein is inserted into your genome'

'However, they've devised a solution: THE vaccination.' Things have already gotten out of hand a few times with studies like the Oxford vaccination (spinal cord inflammation / paralysis). 'Must be conceivable...,' Capel continues, sarcastically. ' But it isn't a vaccine in the least! It's genetic engineering. It's an adenovirus from a chimp that they've tweaked to allow it to infect humans. They cloned the spike protein (the protein that corona interacts to) into that virus. This isn't a vaccine; it's just genetic manipulation.' It was generated in human embryonic kidney cells that had been genetically engineered.

15

'How do they do it?' SARS-Cov-2 is a protein that may be inserted into your genome and expressed in a variety of organs. Then they merely wait for an immunological response to kick in and do anything. However, it has the potential to spiral out of control*. If we also see that human embryos are being utilized for this, and that some tumor genes are being inserted into them to make them develop, we can conclude that this is simply genetic alteration.'

(What's our perspective on it? The next 'pandemic' will be caused by the Covid vaccine, which will be deployed in even more immunization rounds. The ultimate goal: every person on the planet must be vaccinated and so genetically changed on a regular basis, while the "refusers" must be ostracized and eventually eliminated away).*

The entire human race will be genetically modified starting this year.

So, starting this year, the entire human population will be genetically modified on an unprecedentedly large scale over the world. Vaccination is a euphemism for this process. It's not a vaccine; it's a mixture of bacteria or virus proteins or membrane fragments mixed with a lot of garbage to stimulate the immune system. However, if you inject that into the body and it causes a reaction, it will go. The Oxford vaccine, on the other hand, is not a vaccine and will not disappear.'

Human embryos... HUMANS that have been genetically modified...

Because the coronavirus is prone to alterations, it's unclear whether these alterations are also present in the vaccine's spike protein. If that isn't the case (and the chances are quite high, if not near 100 percent), then this 'vaccine' is useless.

As a result, instead of vaccination, a new technology is employed: genetic alteration. There is a lot of misunderstanding about this. Animal testing is omitted with haste, and all sorts of things are yelled about, and this becomes the 'salvation' of everything. ' Capel depicts a dramatic image of an above-ground nuclear test in the 1950s in the United States, with hundreds of soldiers watching from a safe distance. They'd been advised that 'decent sunglasses' would be sufficient protection.. (By the 1970s, almost all of these guys had developed leukemia and other tumors).

Crowd control; mainstream media's monstrous misinformation campaign

'So the procedures are ineffective against the virus, but they are incredibly effective against crowd control.' Those measures are admirable, but for what purpose? It has nothing to do with the virus. In addition, there is a misinformation campaign going on (by the mainstream media, the OMT and the cabinet). We are constantly assaulted with bizarre stories, which makes us all very anxious, and we blindly follow all of the rules. These are having an effect, but on what do they have an effect?'

Control of the populace by a totalitarian regime

So, what are the benefits of lockdowns, 1.5 meters, and mouth caps? In order to maintain totalitarian control over the populace. Then you use all kinds of lies to terrify people. Then you induce massive hardship and misery via lockdowns, such as bankruptcies and famines.'

Then you use facemasks that make no sense at all to instill terror in people to the point where they ask for it. If you enhance people's terror, they will demand more dictatorship, as George Orwell predicted.

Big Pharma - Big Data - Big Banking - Big Reset - Big Scam!

Capel concludes, "I am not a conspiracy theorist." These measures, on the other hand, are prescribed internationally from a single source: the WHO, which is linked to other systems (including Bill Gates' GAVI vaccine partnership). One thing that is obvious is that this 'vaccine,' this genetic manipulation, is generating a significant amount of revenue... The government has previously spent a significant amount of money (hundreds of millions of dollars) on a vaccine that does not exist. This is a substantial sum of money for 'Big Pharma.'

'Then you realize that everyone is required to have an app, which may or may not be 'chipped.' Then there's 'Big Data,' the new gold, and 'Big Banking,' because money flows will be entirely altered (full payment digitalization in / from 2021).

So, how big of a 'Big Reset' and a 'Big Scam' is this? I have to say, this is incredible, and I could never have imagined it even in my wildest dreams.'

'There is a frenzied insistence on these tactics, which work really well for crowd control and societal destabilization, so now we are seeing emergency laws being passed that utterly eliminate democracy.'

Then, in March of the following year, elections will take place, right in the middle of Covid-20 (or Covid-21). Will they then claim that this is why they are unable to call an election?

Chapter 2: Biggest hoax ever?

Dr. Hodkinson, the 20-year president of the biotech company that currently sells Covid-19 tests, cautions that the tests do not demonstrate clinical infection and blames "media and political hysteria."

More and more eminent scientists are speaking out against what is being done in the name of combating the current coronavirus, notably in the West. Dr. Roger Hodkinson, a virologist and pathology specialist, was the former chair of the Royal College of Physicians of Canada's Examination Committee of Pathology in Ottawa, the CEO of a large private medical lab in Edmonton, and the CEO and medical director of Western Medical Assessments, one of the producers of Covid-19 tests, for 20 years. Western's corona policy is "completely unjustified hysteria," according to Dr. Hodkinson, and "the worst scam ever perpetuated upon the naïve people."

Dr. Hodkinson remarked during a recent public video/audio meeting of an Edmonton City Council committee that Covid-19 is "nothing more than a go to flu season." This isn't the Ebola virus. It isn't SARS (-1). It's politics vs. medicine, and that's a hazardous game to play.'

'The simple truth is that the media and politics are fueling a completely baseless public frenzy.' It's ridiculous. This is the biggest ruse ever perpetrated on the general people.'

'Facemasks are absolutely pointless; no further policy is required.'

The scientist emphasized that no further measures are required beyond what is routinely done during a seasonal flu. 'When we were sick, we stayed at home and ate chicken soup instead of going to see Grandma.' We didn't need someone to tell us whether or not we should return to work.'

He claims that mouthguards are absolutely ineffective. 'There is no evidence that they work... (facemasks) are simply there to show that you are virtuous... You see all these people marching around like lemmings, obeying without question and covering their mouths with a mouthguard.'

'Everything needs to reopen tomorrow, and all testing has to halt.'

'At the same time, social separation is futile. Covid is dispersed via aerosols that travel 30 meters* before landing (*possibly 30 feet = roughly 10 meters). The unforeseen repercussions of lockdowns are horrifying! As stated in the (signed by tens of thousands of scientists, medics, and other specialists) Great Barrington Declaration, which I disseminated before to

this meeting, everything should be open again tomorrow.'

'I sell (Covid) tests, but I'd like to highlight with neon letters that positive test results do not imply clinical infection (as the media and politicians fraudulently claim with their statistics of 'infections')! Unless you submit yourself to the hospital with a respiratory ailment, (the tests) merely cause public frenzy and should be stopped...

All we should be doing is protecting the vulnerable and providing 3000 to 5000 I.E. of vitamin D to all nursing home patients every day, as this has been demonstrated to dramatically lower the (risk of) infection.'

'What is being done now is utterly ludicrous.'

'I remind you that according to Alberta's own data, the probability of death for persons under 65 is one in 300,000.' You guys need to get a handle on this. Given the ramifications, the scale of your reaction, which you are undertaking without any evidence, is completely ludicrous. Suicides, company closures, funerals, weddings, and other events abound. It's ridiculous, because it's nothing more than a terrible flu.'

'Let people make their own choice,' Hodkinson concluded, advising governments. You should be completely deafeningly deafeningly deafeningly deafening The provincial director of public health is deceiving you. I'm outraged that it's gotten to this point. It should all come to an end tomorrow.

severe side effects. Until 2019, there was no question that a vaccine should then be labeled as a failure, and thrown in the trash. This year, however, it was decided to continue with the development, and even 1 billion of these vaccines have already been ordered.

97% of women infertile after clinical trial of GSK corona vaccine

American presenter David Knight recently quoted a whistleblower from pharma giant GSK, who revealed that so-called 'anti-HCG' (hormone) adjuvants in corona vaccines cause 97% sterility. In fact, during a clinical trial of the GSK vaccine, 61 out of 63 women were said to have become infertile.

In a variant developed for men with an anti-GNRH (hormone), the testes would shrink, testosterone levels would drop, and the mitochondrial DNA in sperm would be destroyed, causing infertility in women. This was allegedly observed during vaccine tests on baboons.

According to the British spokesman for Govote.org, which Knight showed a video clip of, this will result in masses of people dying from Covid-19 vaccines in the coming years, while virtually no more children will be born. 'If this is their intention, we will have a massive global population reduction, which Bill Gates has been talking about for years.' That's why Govote.org wants the vaccines tested in independent labs.

Chapter 3: Toxic nano particles

Synthetic substance PEG in vaccines increasingly controversial due to violent immune system counter-reactions - 'British GSK whistleblower: Corona vaccines contained adjuvants that rendered 97% women infertile in clinical trial phase'

The ministry in the Eu and several experts in the field of medicine in the united states conceded that the nano particles in the Pfizer vaccine pose a "risk" because they are new technology that has never been in approved vaccines. Nevertheless, the government sees no objection to continuing the supply of this vaccine under the European flag. An American journalist writes that the nano particles are 'potentially lethal', which can only be proven when the vaccine is actually administered to people. Do they really want to let it get this far?

Suppose you are prescribed a new painkiller by your family doctor. When you go to pick it up at the pharmacy, you are told both orally and in writing that there are new substances in this painkiller, the effects of which are only theoretical, and therefore pose an additional risk to you. Are you going to take it anyway? (Of course you say 'no', but the reality of 2021 is that three quarters of the people will probably take it anyway. Just look at how the absurd facemask obligation - in our opinion only meant to psychologically mold people and make them ripe for vaccinations - is blindly followed).

Synthetic substance PEG can cause life-threatening reactions

The Pfizer vaccine must be stored at -70 degrees Celsius, which is extremely cold even for a vaccine. The reason is that otherwise the ingredients decay and stop working. Pfizer claims that this vaccine is '90%' effective, but as we have explained many times, this is nothing more than a case of 'butcher judging his own meat' and 'we of the duck company...'. In short: pure propaganda, not verified by thorough research by independent scientists.

Children's Health Defense of Robert Kennedy Jr. wrote back in August that 'mRNA vaccines undergoing clinical Covid-19 testing, including the Moderna vaccine, are based on a nanoparticle 'transport system' containing a synthetic substance called polyethylene glycol (PEG)... The use of PEG in drugs and vaccines is increasingly controversial because of the well-documented cases of opposing PEG-linked immune reactions, including life-threatening anaphylaxis.'

'Moderna is very well aware of safety risks'

'Roughly 7 out of 10 Americans may already have been sensitized to PEG, which can lead to reduced vaccine efficacy and an increase in opposing side effects. If a

PEG-containing mRNA vaccine is approved for Covid-the increased exposure to PEG will be unprecedented and potentially dangerous.'

Documents and publications show that Moderna is very well aware of the safety risks posed by the use of PEG and other aspects of mRNA technology, but considers its own bottom line more important. At the other pharma giants, including Pfizer, it will be no different. For example, Pfizer was sued in 2007 for causing disabled and dead children as a result of "illegal testing" on some 200 Nigerian children with an anti-rabbit drug.

100% mild to severe side effects in testing phase, yet 1 billion ordered

The LNPs (Lipid Nano Particles) in these vaccines protect the mRNA substances from decay, and enhance uptake into human cells. In addition, they make the immune system work faster, a property that vaccine scientists describe as "inherent adjuvant properties.

Adjuvants are added to vaccines to trigger a (hyper)immune response, so that antibodies are formed. The pharma giants base their claims of '90% (or higher) efficacy' solely on this, and never talk about the established serious adverse reactions (ADRs) that these substances always cause in some people.

In a previous clinical trial phase with the Moderna vaccine, 100% of all participants experienced mild to

(Is this perhaps the real reason that the military intelligence site Deagel has been predicting for years that about three-quarters of the population - meaning hundreds of millions of people - in the U.S. and Europe will be gone by 2025? We first wrote about this in June 2017. See also our article Only 5 more years? Decay of Western Civilization Proceeds Exactly According to 'The Fourth Turning Point' (1997),

These are such shocking claims that more evidence would absolutely have to come to the surface for it to be presented as 'plausible'. Nevertheless, experiences with vaccine manufacturers and the governments that protect them show that we cannot simply trust claims that vaccines are 'proven safe' (think of the swine flu vaccine in 2009).

Self-reinforcing spiral of vaccine deaths, mandatory vaccinations, and more deaths?

'Once people die from the corona vaccines, the medical establishment will call all these deaths 'Covid 19 victims' so they can claim the pandemic is getting worse again,' reads Mike 'Natural News' Adams' fearful suspicion. This will set off a new death cycle, with (even more) hysteria in the media, and mandatory vaccines. These in turn will cause even more deaths,' upon which even more people will be vaccinated and thus more people will die, et cetera.

In the end, the vaccines will probably kill more people than the coronavirus. George Orwell's authoritarian medical nightmare will be a reality as soon as the 'treatment' allows the pandemic to continue indefinitely, and the total scamdemic is used to crush people's freedoms and lock them up like slaves in their own homes all over the world.

'Bill Gates celebrates in advance'

This is what happens when Big Pharma and the deep state conspire to destroy freedom, and work towards their ultimate goal: mass genocide of humanity. Bill Gates will no doubt be celebrating in advance, even before the mass deaths begin,' Adams continued.

'If you want to survive this, resist the corona vaccine at all costs. Defend yourself in every way you can against the vaccine force, or you will perish.'

We by no means dare to state with certainty that Mike Adams is right, and this global genocide is indeed the real underlying plan, but reiterate the ever more pressing question: do you dare take this risk?

Chapter 4: Changing our DNA?

Controversial Pfizer experimental vaccine approved in Britain: 'The benefits far outweigh the drawbacks' - 100 million doses still available this year, 1.3 billion by end of next year

Pfizer, in collaboration with Germany's BioNTech, has developed a Covid vaccine - now approved in the UK - that uses mRNA to program human cells to produce antibodies. This means that an attenuated virus is no longer used. This technology is now being used for the first time in vaccines. For this reason alone, the consequences are completely unpredictable. On top of this, a university scientific team in the USA warns that CRISPR technology, which alters genes, is far from being safe and reliable. On the contrary, experiments have shown that all kinds of unforeseen errors can occur in the body, with potentially enormous consequences, even for the next generations.

A scientific team from Columbia University conducted research on CRISPR technology that allows human genes to be programmed, changed or deleted directly. The study was published in the journal Cell. The inherently laudable goal is to be able to eliminate all kinds of diseases and disorders in the future.

Scientists discovered during experiments with embryos that trying to repair damaged genes that cause hereditary blindness triggers unintended and unwanted changes, often resulting in the partial or even complete elimination of the entire chromosome (DNA).

Top institutes warn of 'potentially dangerous changes'

In September, an international committee sponsored by the U.S. National Academy of Medicine, the National Academy of Sciences and the British Royal Society concluded that the technology used to edit genes (gene editing) is not yet ready to be used on humans because scientists are not yet able to make precise repairs or modifications without causing potentially dangerous changes.

Although the new mRNA vaccines do not do exactly the same thing as the "cut and paste" described above, the basic technology amounts to the same thing: human cells are manipulated, activated and potentially altered directly with programmed genetic material (mRNA). In the Pfizer/BioNTech vaccine, that mRNA is also transported by nano particles (LNPs), which have also never before been approved for use in human vaccines.

Scientific consensus that technology is not yet safe

The Crispr Journal recently published a paper with the views of more than 30 experts regarding the CRISPR gene-editing technology. Which, contrary to what 'Big Pharma', politics and media make it seem, is still controversial in the scientific community because changes made to human genes are passed on to future generations.

Jennifer Doudna, the biochemist who won the Nobel Prize with a colleague this year for her work with CRISPR technology, pointed out that the scientific consensus is that the technology should not be applied to embryos at this time. However, experiments are being conducted or planned in China, Europe and the US on patients suffering from cancer, hereditary blood diseases and other conditions.

In 2018, the birth of twins whose DNA had been altered using CRISPR caused a great deal of concern. Another woman was also reported to have had a genetically modified embryo implanted. It is unknown how the babies fared. Chinese scientist He Jianku was sentenced to 3 years in prison for these illegal medical experiments.

'Entire chromosome lost after CRISPR-Cas treatment'

Researchers in the new study published in Cell used sperm from one man with hereditary blindness to create 40 embryos. Using the CRISPR- Cas9 method, the mutation in the father's DNA was cut out. An enzyme was then inserted into 37 embryos with the intention of fixing the mutation.

What happened: about half of the embryos lost large portions, or even the entire chromosome on which the mutated EYS gene that causes blindness resides. 'This is a very unfavorable result,' admitted Dr. Dieter Egli, senior author of the study. 'The human embryo seems to be unique with its poor ability to repair a break in its DNA.' This biological observation, he said, goes beyond the debate over the use of CRISPR in embryos.

Nearly explicit recognition that 'old vaccines' pose risk of infection

This brings us to the Covid vaccines. 'Our vaccine consists of a short segment of genetic material called messenger RNA, which contains instructions for a human cell to make a harmless version of a 'target' protein, or immunogen, that activates the body's immune response against the SARS-CoV-2 virus,' BioNTech's website states. 'This means that the immune system learns to recognize the SARS-CoV-2 virus after exposure, and then prevents infection.'

With the next sentence, 'Unlike other vaccines, mRNA vaccines do not contain the virus itself, and therefore do not pose a risk of infection', it is almost explicitly admitted that the existing vaccines that have been administered for decades, and which have been claimed to be 'safe' all this time, do pose a risk of contracting the very disease you are supposed to be vaccinated against.

In 2017, the WHO noted that the global polio explosion was primarily caused by vaccines. The very worst epidemics in the Congo, Afghanistan and the Philippines could all be traced to vaccines. In 2018, as many as 70% of all polio cases worldwide were caused by vaccines.

Significant reservations about efficacy and safety

Incidentally, BioNTech - which works closely with China's Fosun Pharma - is not so sure about the efficacy and safety of the new mRNA vaccine itself: 'mRNA vaccines are a powerful new development class of vaccines with potential high versatility and favorable safety properties... We expect that our vaccine approach will stimulate the immune system to generate protective antibodies.'

'BNT162b2 (= the chosen vaccine variant)... encodes an optimized full-length SARS-CoV-2 spike glycoprotein, which is the target of the neutralizing antibodies believed to inactivate the virus.' Surely that's a considerable stretch compared to the 90% efficacy (or higher) that has been so highly acclaimed in the media and is said to have been achieved during the clinical trial phases.

Genetic information SARS-CoV-2 injected directly into your body

In the simplified working diagram posted on the BioNTech website, it is indeed crystal clear that the basis of the new mRNA vaccine is genetic information from the SARS-CoV-2 virus itself. This Covid virus information is transported and protected in nanoparticles, and so injected into your body, whereupon your immune system is confronted with it, in the hope that it will produce the appropriate antibodies.

This does not mean that this information will be introduced into your cells through direct "cutting and pasting," as is done with the CRISPR-Cas9 (and Cas12, and now Cas13) method in embryos and serious diseases, and there change your DNA directly, but it can be done indirectly.

Molecular biologist Borger: It's actually about samRNA

Indeed, molecular biologist Peter Borger, who along with 22 fellow scientists submitted a retraction request for the Drosten/Marion Koopmans paper on which the PCR tests are based, recently explained at Café Weltschmerz that it's actually about samRNA vaccines (sam= 'self amplifying messenger' = self-replicating). You vaccinate with a different kind of virus, from which you have extracted all the virulent genes. But then you put that back into humans with a Covid gene in it.'

'You then get an injection that allows that altered virus to enter your immune system and be taken up. That's a virus-like molecule, which is going to write off the RNA. That RNA is a messenger for a protein, which is made from it. That is then put on the membrane of a cell (for example, muscle cell or immune cell). The immune system can then develop a response to that.'

'You can indeed be genetically altered'

'Nice method, but on the other hand it's a self-amplifying molecule, so you get a very high concentration of these kinds of RNAs in your cells. What the developers didn't realize is that a high concentration of viral RNA that they inserted can be turned into DNA by a certain reaction, and then put back into your own genome.'

'You do often hear that we are being genetically altered by these kinds of new vaccines, but we never get to hear how that happens. Well, this is the way that that can happen... It doesn't have to happen, but it can, it's not out of the question, because they haven't done any research on that. It's possible for an RNA molecule to be converted into a DNA molecule, and then randomly put back into your genome somewhere.'

'You can imagine that then ... over time you start to have certain side effects. Eventually even the immune system or the metabolic system can be affected, because somewhere a mutation has occurred in your DNA. That's then that piece of the virus that has been put back into your genome.'

1.3 billion doses by end of next year; Brits approve vaccine

Investigative journalist Martin Vrijland has been writing for quite some time (well before the corona 'pandemic') about the RNA/DNA changing CRISPR technology that seems to be put into the new vaccines, and predicted as early as April 23 that BioNTech might (co) supply that vaccine. (For more info: read, among other things, his November 11 article "BioNTech is going to deliver the CRISPR online read-and-write 'vaccine' that can program your DNA predicted here.")

By the end of 2020, 100 million doses of this potentially DNA-altering Pfizer/BioNTech vaccine should be made, and a year later, more than 1.3 billion. It was announced today that the vaccine has been approved in Great Britain because "the benefits far outweigh the drawbacks," according to Dr. June Raine of the government medical agency MHRA.

We, on the other hand, already feel sorry for all those people around the world who are eager to have this highly experimental good injected into their bodies, because they yearn for life to return to normal afterwards.

Chapter 5: Women become infertile?

Based on these official documents, women who wish to have children should think twice about being vaccinated against Covid-19 -British Government Committee on Vaccination and Immunization: "Pregnancy should be ruled out before vaccinating, and we have not studied interactions with other medication"

The leaflets and care instructions for the Pfizer/BioNTech 'nano' mRNA vaccine, which will be administered to the UK population from next week, explicitly warn not to give the vaccine to children under 16 and pregnant women: 'Before vaccinating, pregnancy should be excluded.' People with weakened defenses-who have not participated in the clinical trial phases-and those who take medications regularly are 'advised' to contact a doctor first. Women who have the vaccine injected should take care not to become pregnant for the first 2 months after the second dose, which must be taken 21 days after the first.

You may be saying: these warnings aren't that abnormal, are they? They are also found in most package inserts of regular medicines. Indeed, they are. However, these are drugs intended for people suffering from a disease or condition, not for healthy people, all of whom should now receive a Covid vaccine.

The Joint Committee on Vaccination and Immunization has advised pregnant women and women who want to become pregnant not to take the vaccine at all. This means that the vaccine is simply not considered safe for these groups.

'No interaction studies with other medicinal products'

Caregivers are given the special warning in these instructions that medics and equipment should be kept ready "in case of a rare anaphylactic event following administration of the vaccine. We recently reported that official documents show that the British government, however, expects "a high number" of serious adverse reactions, so-called A.D.R.'s (Adverse Drug Reactions). A.D.R.'s include serious illness, long-term or permanent illness and disability, and deaths.

'As with any vaccine, vaccination with Covid-19 mRNA vaccine BNT162b2 does not protect all vaccine recipients. No data are available on the use of this vaccine in persons who have previously received a full or partial series with another Covid-19 vaccine.' In addition, 'no interaction studies (with other medicinal products) have been conducted.' It will be clear why we underlined this, because in Germany alone, millions of people take one or more medications every day.

There are quite a few over-16s who experienced 'mild to moderate' side effects during the test phases: 80+% had pain at the site of vaccination, 60+% experienced fatigue, 50+% headaches, 30+% muscle aches, 30+% chills, 20+% joint pain, and 10+% fever. These side effects "usually went away a few days after vaccination. Redness and swelling of the injection site and nausea were also among the "frequent" side effects.

No testing with people with weakened immune system

People with demonstrably weakened immune systems were excluded from the clinical trial phases. In the second phase, although 40% of the test subjects were people over 56, the statistics actually show that Covid-19 poses hardly any danger to people up to 70 (WHO confirmed IFR of only 0.05%). Have people over 70 been tested at all? Presumably not, as most of them have weakened or even non-functioning immune systems.

In fact, the UK government itself is not even sure the vaccine will work: 'The vaccine elicits both neutralizing antibodies and a cellular immune response to the spike (S) antigen, which may help protect against Covid-19 disease.' (bold and underlined added). This alone cancels out the average 95% efficacy during the clinical trial phases also reported in these instructions. That percentage is also based on the PCR test, now totally debunked for this purpose, which was used to test participants in both the vaccinated group and the placebo group to see if they had become 'infected'.

Unknown what the effects are on human fertility and development

But it doesn't stop here. The instructions to health care providers literally state that "it is unknown whether the Covid-19 mRNA vaccine BNT162b2 affects fertility. So that means that there is a chance that this vaccine may make you infertile.

At 4.6 'Fertility, pregnancy and lactation' it is stated that 'there is no, or a limited amount of data from the use of Covid-19 mRNA vaccine. Animal reproductive toxicity studies have not been completed. Covid-19 mRNA vaccine BNT162b2 is not recommended during pregnancy. For women of childbearing age, pregnancy should be excluded before vaccination. In addition, women who may give birth to children should be advised to avoid pregnancy for at least 2 months after their second dose.'

Under section 5.3 'Preclinical safety data' it is reaffirmed that 'Non-clinical data show no special hazard for humans based on a conventional study with repeated doses of toxicity. Animal studies of potential toxicity to reproduction and development have not been completed.' (emphasis added)

Let this sink in for a moment.

The animal trials to see if this vaccine has any effects on reproduction, i.e. reproduction, and development, have not even been completed. This means that we have no idea (yet?) whether this vaccine will affect the reproduction and development of anyone who receives

41

it. Or perhaps they do have an idea, and were so shocked by the results that they decided not to even complete the tests on animals?

Alleged GSK whistleblower: 'Vaccine caused 97% sterility in test phase'

On November 21, we wrote in our article "Nano particles in Pfizer vaccine according to minister De Jonge 'risk', but vaccine will be there anyway": American presenter David Knight recently cited a whistleblower from pharma giant GSK (link works again), who revealed that so-called 'anti-HCG' (hormone) adjuvants in corona vaccines cause 97% sterility. Indeed, during a clinical trial of the GSK vaccine, 61 out of 63 women were reported to have become infertile.

In a variant developed for men with an anti-GNRH (hormone), the testes would shrink, testosterone levels would drop, and the mitochondrial DNA in sperm would be destroyed, causing infertility in women. This was allegedly observed during vaccine tests on baboons.

According to the British spokesman for Govote.org, which Knight showed a video clip of, this will result in masses of people dying from Covid-19 vaccines in the coming years, while virtually no more children will be born. 'If this is their intention, we will have a massive global population reduction, which Bill Gates has been talking about for years.' That's why Govote.org wants the vaccines tested in independent laboratories.

'Vaccine can attack essential protein in women making them infertile'

The mRNA vaccines are going to program the body itself to make antibodies against the 'spike' protein of the SARS-CoV-2 virus. The now following unconfirmed information about this needs further study and verification: 'Spike proteins also contain syncytin homologous protien, which are essential for the formation of the placenta in mammals such as humans. It should be absolutely ruled out that a vaccine against SARS-CoV-2 can trigger an immune response against syncytin-1, because otherwise infertility of indefinite duration may occur in vaccinated women.'

'The vaccine contains a spike protein called syncytin-1, vital for the formation of human placenta in women. If it (vaccine) works and we thus form an immune response against the spike protein, we are also training the female body to attack syncytin-1, which can lead to infertility in women.

Since these vaccines are forced on us, but nevertheless you are given full responsibility in advance if things go wrong, this therefore means that IF you as a woman or man do indeed become infertile because of this vaccine, you are entirely to blame. After all, the manufacturers and medical authorities are already not holding

43

themselves liable for this. Nevertheless, you will soon be punished if you refuse these vaccinations, and you may be denied access to airplanes, buildings, stores and events. And that will probably only be the beginning of the total social and societal exclusion.

Chapter 6: Vaccine death numbers rising?

In one week, 700 Americans dead after vaccination against Covid-19; 2190 heart attacks, and already 4,583 people disabled after their vaccine; 652 women miscarried - Delta variant Great Britain: more than 2x as many deaths among vaccinated than among unvaccinated in percentage terms - 'American companies count on losing HALF of their vaccinated employees in the next 3 years'

As in India, Chile, Taiwan and the Seychelles, the number of deaths has also exploded in the US and Great Britain after the start of the mass vaccination campaign against Covid-19. In less than 5 months, there have been more official vaccine deaths in the US than in the past 10 years (!). According to the VAERS registration system - which historically records only 1% to a maximum of 10% of the actual number of cases - over 1750 people died from vaccines in the first 3 months. That number currently stands at 5997. In the past week alone, 700 people died after being vaccinated against Covid-19.

Already 19,597 people were hospitalized after being vaccinated. 15,052 people had a severe allergic reaction. Another 43,891 people needed emergency medical attention. 2190 people had a heart attack, 1564 had thrombosis / blood clots / too low a level of platelets, 652 women had a miscarriage, and 4583 people were disabled.

More than 2 times as many deaths among vaccinated people

A 'vax horror massacre' is also taking place in Great Britain. The figures (Public Health England / UK National Health Service) are staggering: the number of deaths among vaccinated people is twice as high in percentage terms as among unvaccinated people.

Of the 19,573 unvaccinated who would have received the "delta" variant - which the mainstream media is of course again exploiting for yet another fear terror campaign - 23 people died (= mortality rate 0.00117%), including the "unlinked" category (4289 cases, bringing mortality rate to 0.00096%).

Of the 9344 vaccinated who received the delta mutation, 19 died (= mortality rate 0.00246%), more than twice as high as the unvaccinated, and more than 2.5 times as high if the 'unlinked' cases are also included. 7 of the 19 deceased vaccinees died after 21 days or more after their first injection, and 12 of them died 14 days or more after their second shot, directly implicating the vaccine as a direct cause.

Warnings experts were ignored

The trend confirms the warnings of numerous scientists and experts such as the professor Pierre Capel, who has been warning since the autumn of 2020 that exactly this was about to happen what is now visible in more and more countries: vaccinated people who are subsequently infected with the virus or a mutation are much more likely than unvaccinated people to get ADE (Antibody Dependent Enhancement), a consequent serious illness or even death.

Celebrated scientists such as HIV-discoverer and Nobel laureate Luc Montagnier, and in Europe, Professor Schetters, have hammered away in vain at the fact that until 2020 it was an undisputed scientific fact that vaccinating during a pandemic is the most stupid thing you can ever do, because you create potentially dangerous mutations, which in turn increases the number of sick and dead.

However, politics never seemed to be about health or safety, but about injecting everyone as enforced as possible with experimental genetically modified organisms / gene therapy, as part of the technocratic transhuman totalitarian control agenda now being imposed on the world's population under various names (Great Reset, Agenda-2030, Build Back Better, Green New Deal).

'American companies count on losing MANY of their vaccinated employees'

American radio host Hal Turner has posted a video for subscribers that purports to show that American companies are counting on losing HALF of their vaccinated employees to a Covid-19 vaccine (dead or disabled). This information cannot be verified at this time.

vaccination will continue as usual. The only consideration is to give children up to 20 years of age only one shot, or to reduce the dose, or to lengthen the time between injections.

'Congratulations, you are destroying ALL confidence in ALL vaccines for a generation'

Berenson, author of "Tell Your Children: The Truth about Marijuana, Mental Illness and Violence," among other books, is appalled at the authorities: "Congratulations, you morons. You are about to destroy a generation's worth of ALL confidence in ALL vaccines and ALL public health measures.'

Well, that trust has long since disappeared in a growing number of people, Mr. Berenson, as evidenced by the fact that Americans have had to be persuaded lately with free lotto tickets, bonuses and all sorts of prize festivals to go get their 'shots.

Berens analyzed all the statistics, concluding that the incidence of heart disease among children and adolescents is as much as 40 times higher than normal. 'And consider that most side effects are not reported, even if they are serious.'

The author writes of being behind a lawsuit by a student who is suing his private school for demanding that all students be vaccinated against Covid-19. One reader has reportedly already offered $25,000 in

51

support. Across the U.S., numerous schools and universities are already mandating vaccinations.

Israel: 275 cases

On the same day (June 1), the Israeli Ministry of Health reported 275 cases of heart infection (again, mostly young men aged 16 - 30) out of more than 5 million vaccinations. This may seem small, but the same misleading registration system is used here: only people who become ill shortly after their vaccination are counted, even though it has long been scientifically known that people can become ill as a result of vaccinations several months or even years later.

Chapter 8: Vaccine restrictions?

Air travel for ordinary people has been a thorn in the side of the globalist climate-vaccine cult for years. Now, it seems, steps are actually being taken to put an end to it once and for all under the guise of "health" and "safety. Vaccinated people have increased risk of brain hemorrhage or heart attack and European pilots are locked in hotel rooms despite vaccinations.

Airlines in Spain and Russia have begun to warn vaccinated people not to get on a plane. They may even be hit with a no-fly zone. The reason is that vaccinated people are at extra risk of blood clots (DVT: Deep Vein Thrombosis) in high-altitude pressurized cabins, and can therefore suffer a brain hemorrhage or heart attack more quickly.

The US CDC has a general warning on its website for people who travel longer than four hours by plane: "More than 300 million people travel annually on long-haul flights (usually more than four hours). Blood clots, also called DVT (deep vein thrombosis), can be a serious risk for some long-distance travelers... Anyone who travels for more than four hours, whether by plane, car, bus or train, may be at risk of blood clots.

The end for almost ALL travel?

That the car, bus and train have now been added to that list (in which there are no pressurized cabins) makes many people wonder whether the globalist climate-vaccine sect intends, under the guise of 'health' and 'the climate', to put an end to almost ALL travel (except for themselves, of course).

Initially, the plan was to allow only vaccinated people to have access to international flights again. Now that it turns out that they are actually at increased risk, the question arises whether it was indeed not the intention from the outset to put an end to at least 90% of air travel.

Pilots are locked up in hotel rooms despite vaccinations

Despite their vaccinations, pilots and other crew members in Europe are locked in hotel rooms immediately upon arrival at an airport. In most cases, they are not allowed to leave the airport. In March, the European Aviation Safety Agency (EASA) recommended that vaccinated pilots also be quarantined for at least two days before boarding.

Since vaccinated pilots spend much longer "in the air" and they are therefore at even greater risk, this raises the question of whether air travel has not become permanently more unsafe.

Australian airlines deny there is greater risk

American economist Martin Armstrong writes of having a friend who was vaccinated against Covid, and then suffered a blood clot that he had to have surgically removed.

According to the UK Evening Standard, the risk is the same for vaccinated and unvaccinated people. Australian airlines claim it's not true at all, and you can just fly if you're vaccinated. 'Of course they are not interested in people's safety,' Armstrong responds. 'They just want to stay afloat. There have been recorded deaths from blood clots after people were vaccinated, without flying. Others have found that Covid deaths often had blood clots.'

'Politicians will never admit their mistakes; there is no one left whom we can trust'

'As with everything around Covid, there is no real hard information. We probably won't get any either, because the government is pushing the vaccine through. Politicians will NEVER admit their mistakes, no matter how many people die. They can't be prosecuted, because they control the whole (judicial) process, and the media doesn't help either.'

Armstrong writes that he would rather remain normal. *'If I never have to leave my house again - fine. I've had enough of this deranged world anyway. I will patiently wait for the mushroom cloud that removes the threat to*

*humanity and signals that it is all over. There is simply
no one left in the authorities whom we can trust.'*

Chapter 9: The US and China working together?

Why did China NOT use the challenged mRNA/DNA technology in its own vaccines? - NIH director: 'SARS-1 and MERS also come from there'

And yet another 'conspiracy theory' that turns out to be a hard fact, thereby exposing yet another lie perpetuated for months by the mainstream media and politicians. Dr. Francis Collins, the current director of the American National Institutes of Health (NIH), has frankly admitted in an interview that the Americans and the Chinese collaborated to make the coronavirus more contagious to humans ('gain of function') in the biohazard-4 lab in Wuhan. Dr. Anthony Fauci, who is in ever greater trouble because of his many lies that have now been proven, denied to the Senate in March that he and his colleague Collins had funded the "gain of function" research in the Wuhan lab. Now he appears to have committed perjury about that.

'SARS and MERS come from there'

Collins' statements are also highly incriminating for Dr. Peter Daszak, who through his Ecohealth Alliance received substantial grants from the NIH to fund the 'gain of function' research in Wuhan. Collins explained in detail how the NIH and the Wuhan Institute of Virology work together. He insisted that there is 'good reason' for this, as both SARS-1 and MERS 'originated there'.

Mike 'Natural News' Adams hears in this that both SARS and MERS come from the Wuhan laboratory, but in my opinion by 'there' Collins meant China in general. Indeed, SARS-1 first surfaced in China in 2003. Its spread was subsequently limited to four other countries.

However, MERS was first detected in Saudi Arabia in 2012 (see also our article yesterday: Medical journals announce potential new pandemic: MERS-CoV). Adams is therefore right to wonder, after all, if "Collins has more information that these relatively new and deadly coronaviruses (SARS, MERS) both came from the Wuhan lab?

Conspiracy theory turns out to be hard fact

Dr. Collins, Daszak and Fauci worked directly with the infamous 'bat lady' Dr. Shi Zhengli, who is funded and rewarded by the Chinese Communist Party (CCP), according to press reports from the Wuhan lab. The Wuhan Institute of Virology is also the center of a 'United Front Group' established to neutralize all potential opposition and criticism of the CCP. When the lab was identified as a possible source of the coronavirus last year, China blocked a WHO investigation into it. Then, for months, Dr. Fauci proclaimed the now-proven crystal-clear lies, and even committed perjury about it.

The same applies to Dr. Daszak, regularly quoted in Western media, who kept insisting that an artificial origin of the virus, i.e. a "lab leak" - intentional or otherwise - was a "conspiracy theory". Scientists who pointed out the many inconsistencies and factual evidence that the bat soup or seafood market theory, also accepted as 'true' in Europe, is pure nonsense, were virulently attacked and blackened. This even happened to HIV-discoverer and Nobel Prize winner Luc Montagnier.

Walking 'COVID factories'

Fauci, Daszak and other system scientists have also gone all out to inject the entire world population with experimental genetic manipulation "vaccines," which have now been shown to turn people into walking "spike factories" that are also "shed" (exhaled) into the environment. In previous articles we pointed out the growing number of scientific studies and reports that those exhaled 'spikes' can also cause damage to the health of unvaccinated people.

If that is placed in the light of the leaked 'Fauci Files', from which it emerged that the coronavirus was already referred to internally as a deliberately created 'bioweapon' on March 11, 2020, then a terrifying picture emerges that is probably too much for most people to take in all at once.

Chinese vaccines contain no mRNA - why not there, and here?

Consider the following: soon after the outbreak of the corona pandemic, China shared all the information about the (supposed) SARS-CoV-2 virus with the world, including the complete genetic construction plan. Based on this, new vaccines based on mRNA and DNA technology, never used or tested on humans, were developed in America, Europe, Russia and India, with which the largest medical experiment in history is now being conducted by injecting as many people and even children as possible with it.

However, the Chinese vaccines do not contain this mRNA/DNA technology. There, the society and economy have been running normally for quite some time. What could be the reason that the Chinese did not want to inject mRNA instructions into their population? Were they perhaps fully aware of the gigantic risks that would entail?

An even more important question: why was and is it done here?

Chapter 10: No escape?

Member of Canadian government unveiled global roadmap to totalitarian communism in October 2020 in which no one owns anything and everyone must be compulsorily vaccinated!

Yet another country confirming a particularly worrying trend: after the start of the Covid-19 vaccination campaign, the number of sick and dead explodes in Taiwan. The same thing happened before in India, Chile and Seychelles, among others, where more (AstraZeneca) shots were handed out than people live, after which there were 146 times more deaths in 4 months than from corona last year. And as we have been predicting for so long, the authorities refuse to point to the vaccines as the cause, no matter how obvious the statistical link. But the "vaccines" - excuse: experimental genetic gene therapy/manipulation - are now declared untouchable and sacrosanct, and so it is indeed claimed that it is due to a mutation.

Taiwan was rid of corona early this year. Hardly anyone died from Covid-19 anymore, there were hardly any sick people, and life returned to normal - except for the wretched mouth masks, which still had to be worn in public places. The reason for this can only be guessed at, as there was no medical one.

Despite the fact that the umpteenth respiratory virus was under control, the government still began a massive vaccination campaign. This got off to a very slow start in mid-March, but starting in May, the number of people getting injected with experimental mRNA/DNA manipulation suddenly skyrocketed.

EXACTLY at that moment the number of 'cases' and deaths also skyrocketed.

Member of Canadian government revealed road map to totalitarian communism in October

American radio host Hal Turner cites an October 2020 open letter from a member of the Canadian government, which we also published at the time. Here again the most important parts from it:

'I want to give you very important information. I am a committee member of the Liberal Party of Canada. I sit on various committee groups, but the information I give comes from the Strategic Plan Committee (which is controlled by the PMO).' That is the office of left-liberal Prime Minister Justin Trudeau, whose parliament has now given itself unlimited power and an unlimited term without an election as long as there is still a 'pandemic'. Trudeau has thus become Canada's de facto first dictator.

'They have made it very clear that nothing can stop their planned outcome. The roadmap and objectives were drawn up by the prime minister, and go as follows:' (planned time period: late 2020 - late 2021)

* 'Introduce second lockdown restrictions gradually. Start with major urban areas first, and then expand;

* Obtain or build isolation facilities in each province at a rapid pace;

* Rapidly increase the number of new 'Covid cases' and 'Covid deaths' so that there is no longer sufficient testing capacity;

* Complete and total second lockdown in 2021, which is much more severe than the first in spring 2020;

* Present the PLANNED Covid-19 mutation or 'reinfection' with a second virus (possibly called Covid-21 (or perhaps SARS-3 or MERS-CoV)), leading to a THIRD wave with a much higher mortality rate and even higher infection rate;

* The health care system is flooded with Covid-19 / Covid-21 patients;

* THIRD lockdown with even stricter measures, such as a complete stop on ALL travel (second/third quarter 2021);

* Implement universal basic income (for the tens of millions of new unemployed who will lose their jobs permanently as a result of this policy. This UBI will be

completely digital, only allowing you to stay alive and watch TV);

* Supply lines collapse, major shortages (stores, supermarkets, online, etc.), major economic instability, followed by chaos, panic, and total dislocation;

* Deploy the military, and establish checkpoints on all major roads. Travel permanently extremely restricted (only by pass / permission). (Third / fourth quarter 2021).'

Depending on the geopolitical situation, the timeline could still change (e.g., 2021 could also be 2022 or 2023), but 'we have been told that in order to initiate this actual economic collapse on an international scale, the federal government is going to offer Canadians a total debt cancellation.' But that comes at a very high price: anyone who claims it gives up forever all rights to all forms of property, and commits to taking all vaccinations offered.

Refusers will initially have to live under very strict lockdown restrictions indefinitely, and thus stay home permanently. But that will only last for a short period, because once the majority of citizens have made the "transition" (to permanent slavery under a global totalitarian communist and transhumanist control system), "the refusers will be characterized as a threat to public safety, and moved to isolation facilities. **Or, in other words, to concentration camps.**

There they will be given one last chance to still 'participate' in the program and have all vaccinations injected into them. If not, they will remain locked up permanently and lose all their possessions and rights. 'In the end, the Prime Minister implied that this whole agenda will be pushed through, regardless of whether we agree with it or not. And this is not just happening in Canada. All countries will have similar roadmaps and agendas. They want to take advantage of the situation to make large-scale changes' (a financial reset with IMF world currency, the 'Great Reset', 'Build Back Better', UN Agenda 2030, the 'Green New Deal').

After the purposefully initiated economic collapse, many of the tens of millions of unemployed system followers will be eager for a BOA-Sturmabteilung brown shirt job in the government, after which they will impose the above scenario on unwilling fellow citizens with ruthless cruelty. Friends, neighbors, colleagues, family and relatives, students and schoolchildren will betray each other "for the greater good," and will be happy that the "threats to their health" will be cleared away for good. (See also: This is how Reichsmarschall Göring got the people to say, "Scare them and tell them that refusers are a danger") and Corona policy tears families and friends apart, exactly as was done in GDR).

Precisely because most people still refuse to believe that this can and will never happen again, that we are more civilized nowadays and will never again commit such atrocities, it threatens to happen again. The only thing that can stop this whole process, this preconceived perfidious plan, is a massive awareness, followed by a massive (but we repeat: definitely non-violent!) NO.

Chapter 11: The next pandemic?

MERS-CoV had a 40% mortality rate in 2012 - African variant made contagious to humans through genetic engineering - Repeat of 2020, supplemented by mandatory testing and mandatory vaccinations for all? - Predictable: politics and media will blame unvaccinated people

Exactly according to the scenario we have described many times since last year, medical journals are announcing the next pandemic now that Covid-19 seems to be on its way out: MERS-CoV. We can therefore expect a repeat of everything from last year's deliberate scare-mongering to the disinformation propaganda in the mainstream media and a rush to the health care system, after which 'natural' measures will be taken such as new strict lockdowns, supplemented by mandatory testing and mandatory vaccinations for everyone. Because again, the main intention of this pandemic seems to be to inject everyone with yet another series of new experimental vaccines.

'Make no mistake, this will not be the last time the world faces the threat of a pandemic,' Tedros told the UN General Assembly of the health ministers of the 194 member states earlier this year. 'It is an evolutionary certainty that there will be another virus with the potential to be even more infectious and deadly than this one.'

Indeed, that other virus could already be coming. An international team of researchers has discovered that Middle East Respiratory Syndrome (MERS) is just a few mutations away from becoming a serious pandemic. In their paper, published in Proceedings of the National Academy of Sciences, they describe their research on several MERS variants.

MERS-CoV first surfaced in Saudi Arabia in 2012, and is said to be particularly deadly. About 40% of the first patients died from their infections, which were allegedly caused mainly by infected dromedaries. And coincidence or not, evidence was also found that bats had infected the camels. According to researchers, 80% of all dromedaries tested (70% live in Africa) now have antibodies in their blood.

African variant made contagious to humans through genetic engineering

The outbreak of MERS-CoV did not receive much attention because there would be no human-to-human contamination. The scientists investigated why not many more Africans - given their many interactions with dromedaries - had not become infected. There, the virus circulates primarily in dromedaries in Morocco, Nigeria, Ethiopia and Burkina Faso. Samples were collected and it turned out that the variants that occur in Arabia can be easily transmitted from person to person, but not those in Africa.

The difference between the variants is in the amino acids of the S protein. By genetically modifying the African variant so that it had the same 'Arabian' amino acids, they succeeded in making the African variant more infectious to human cells as well. The big, unasked question, of course, is: why would you want to do that? Why would you want to make a virus that is (almost) harmless to humans much more infectious, as happened with the coronavirus?

Anyway, the researchers think that the reason that the variants in the Middle East have not yet mutated to infect many people is that the dromedary trade goes almost exclusively one way, from Africa to the Middle East. However, they warn that if that trade reverses at some point, or if another animal also becomes a carrier and is traded to Africa, mutations could occur that could cause a deadly pandemic. (1)

Virus in top 10 WHO

MERS-CoV is very similar to SARS-1 and also causes very severe respiratory symptoms. Among humans, it still has a 35% mortality rate. There is no treatment or vaccine yet. Since 2012, more than 2,100 people have been infected with MERS-CoV, 813 of whom have died. The virus is now in the top 10 of WHO's list of emerging diseases that should be investigated with the highest priority (2).

SPARS = MERS-CoV or SARS-3?

Late last year, the possible successor to Covid-19 was already announced: SPARS. In a simulation by Johns Hopkins University, this pandemic breaks out in 2025, and lasts until 2028.

'The SPARS pandemic 2025 - 2028; A Futuristic Scenario for Public Health Risk Communicators' (PDF, 2017) was a simulation similar to the later 'Event 201' in October 2019, when every detail was practiced on managing a global outbreak with a coronavirus, which, according to the working forecast, would kill 65 million people. That 'simulation', as you all know, became a reality in almost every respect (only the number of deaths, fortunately, remains far behind (yet?)).

In fact, a World Bank document states that the current 'project' called 'Covid-19 Strategic Preparedness and Response Program (SPRP)' will last until March 31, 2025. Only then will SARS-CoV-2 / Covid-19 presumably be declared definitively 'over', although Covid could therefore also be succeeded by MERS-CoV in the meantime.

After that the successor could start to appear immediately: SPARS, which is a reference to the U.S. city of St.Paul where this future coronavirus will first emerge according to the simulation. This new virus will, of course, be renamed in or around 2025, and could also start again in Asia, for example. However, it could also become SARS-3, which is already ready in an Italian laboratory.

So it is not unlikely that SPARS will actually become SARS-3 or MERS-CoV. 2025 was just a fictional year, which could just as easily become 2023 or earlier. The SPARS simulation also talked about a vaccine called COROVAX as the desired solution to stop this "pandemic," and which would be introduced in the scenario in July 2026. Three years after this 2017 document, a COROVAX vaccine was literally being developed.

This is how anti-vaxxers would be convinced

A notable similarity to SARS-CoV-2 / Covid-19 is that the fictional SPARS infection (/ MERS-CoV or SARS-3 infection?) is often followed by severe bacteriological pneumonia (pg. 57). It also describes how a well-known anti-vaxxer "sees the light" after her infant son develops severe pneumonia, and heals only after administration of regular medication. Authorities then use stories like this to convince vaccine opponents.

Striking similarity to 2020-2021: '... several influential politicians and representatives of institutions came under fire for sensationalizing the severity of the event for certain political gain... A broad social media movement, led mainly by outspoken parents of affected children, coupled with the widespread distrust of 'Big Pharma', supported the narrative that the development of SPARS MCMs (vaccines) was unnecessary, and driven by some profit-seeking individuals.'

It also pointed to 'conspiracy theories' that this virus was also intentionally created, and/or deliberately unleashed on the population by the government as a bioweapon (pg. 66). Meanwhile, the 'Fauci Files', published even by American mainstream media, revealed that the coronavirus was internally called a deliberately created bioweapon as early as March 11, 2020.

Unvaccinated will soon be blamed directly

The pharmaceutical manufacturers, who have proven over the past year how extremely profitable vaccinating during a p(l)andemic can be, are busy developing new vaccines. Bloomberg pointed to GlaxoSmithKline (and partner Sanofi) in late May, which is already making the next generation of Covid vaccines. According to Roger Connor, head of vaccine development, a trial period of a new vaccine on more than 37,000 people was to begin as early as June.

Given the increasingly harsh, often shocking reactions in society to people refusing to be vaccinated against Covid-19 (calls for forced vaccinations are getting louder, and the first calls to put refusers in camps have also been heard), we think that we are long past the stage of "convincing" anti-vaxxers, and soon, if this next pandemic does indeed come, will go straight to openly falsely blaming unvaccinated people by politicians and media.

Suppose that vaccines will indeed cause enormous health problems, as top scientists and other experts have been predicting for months (see our many articles on this subject). Then there will be a new run on health care and hospitals, after which harsh measures will again be taken. On TV, 'scientists' approved by the pharma-vaccine complex will claim that it is not because of the vaccines, but because of a mutation that was able to emerge thanks to the unvaccinated people.

Our other books

Check out our other books for other unreported news, exposed facts and debunked truths, and more.

Join the exclusive Rebel Press Media Circle!

You will get new updates about the unreported reality delivered in your inbox every Friday.

Sign up here today:

https://campsite.bio/rebelpressmedia

CPSIA information can be obtained
at www.ICGtesting.com
Printed in the USA
BVHW080956180821
614615BV00016B/1219